SandCastle

Compound Words

base + ball =
baseball

Amanda Rondeau

Consulting Editor Monica Marx, M.A./Reading Specialist

ABDO
Publishing Company

Published by SandCastle™, an imprint of ABDO Publishing Company, 8000 West 78th Street, Edina, Minnesota 55439.

Printed in the United States of America, North Mankato, Minnesota.
012004   012011

Credits
Edited by: Pam Price
Curriculum Coordinator: Nancy Tuminelly
Cover and Interior Design and Production: Mighty Media
Photo Credits: Brand X Pictures, Comstock, Corbis Images, Eyewire Images, Hemera, PhotoDisc, Rubberball Productions, Stockbyte

Library of Congress Cataloging-in-Publication Data

Rondeau, Amanda, 1974-
    Base + ball = baseball / Amanda Rondeau.
      p. cm. -- (Compound words)
    Includes index.
    Summary: Illustrations and easy-to-read text introduce compound words related to sports and recreation.
    ISBN 1-59197-430-5
    1. English language--Compound words--Juvenile literature. [1. English language--Compound words.] I. Title: Base plus ball equals baseball. II. Title.

PE1175.R66 2003
428.1--dc21

                                                                                              2003048007

SandCastle™ books are created by a professional team of educators, reading specialists, and content developers around five essential components that include phonemic awareness, phonics, vocabulary, text comprehension, and fluency. All books are written, reviewed, and leveled for guided reading, early intervention reading, and Accelerated Reader® programs and designed for use in shared, guided, and independent reading and writing activities to support a balanced approach to literacy instruction.

Let Us Know

After reading the book, SandCastle would like you to tell us your stories about reading. What is your favorite page? Was there something hard that you needed help with? Share the ups and downs of learning to read. We want to hear from you! To get posted on the ABDO Publishing Company Web site, send us e-mail at:

sandcastle@abdopub.com

SandCastle Level: Transitional

A compound
word is two
words joined
together to
make a new
word.

base + ball =

baseball

Coach Wilson
shows Joe and Tom
the right way to
hold a baseball.

soft + ball =

softball

Trish plays outfield on her softball team.

ball + park =

ballpark

Al plays baseball
at the ballpark with
his team.

basket + ball =

basketball

Carla plays basketball after school.

cheer + leader =

cheerleader

Haley likes being a cheerleader.

pop + corn =

popcorn

Ken and Scott like
to eat popcorn at
the movies.

Rusty Wins the Ballgame

Ben takes his dog Rusty
to the ballpark.

When the cheerleaders yell, Rusty
begins to bark.

A player hits the baseball.

Rusty runs out of the grandstand.

He knocks over some popcorn.

He doesn't hear Ben's command.

Rusty runs into the outfield when the batter starts to run.

Rusty jumps over the fence and fetches the ball!

What fun!

More Compound Words

backboard	lineup
ballplayer	quarterback
baseman	scoreboard
batboy	scorekeeper
batgirl	shortstop
dugout	strikeout
football	touchdown
fullback	volleyball
hopscotch	

Glossary

ballpark   a field or stadium where baseball is played

baseball   a sport played with a bat and ball on a field with four bases; the ball used to play baseball

cheerleader   someone who leads the cheering of fans at a sporting event

command   an order

grandstand   the roofed seating area of a stadium for watching a sports event

outfield   the part of a baseball field outside of the bases and inside the foul lines

About SandCastle™

A professional team of educators, reading specialists, and content developers created the SandCastle™ series to support young readers as they develop reading skills and strategies and increase their general knowledge. The SandCastle™ series has four levels that correspond to early literacy development in young children. The levels are provided to help teachers and parents select the appropriate books for young readers.

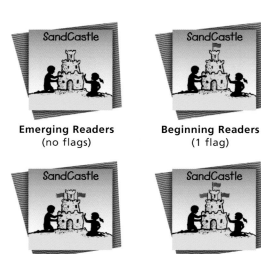

Emerging Readers
(no flags)

Beginning Readers
(1 flag)

Transitional Readers
(2 flags)

Fluent Readers
(3 flags)

These levels are meant only as a guide. All levels are subject to change.

ABDO
Publishing Company

To see a complete list of SandCastle™ books and other nonfiction titles from ABDO Publishing Company, visit **www.abdopublishing.com** or contact us at:

8000 West 78th Street, Edina, Minnesota 55439 • 1-800-800-1312 • fax: 1-952-831-1632